Subcons

MW00917709

Strengthen Your Subconscious Mind Muscle

Tame, Reprogram & Control Your Subconscious Mind to Transform Your Life

Introduction

'You will put your success on autopilot when you learn how to turn your subconscious mind on and make it work towards a desired state of future.'- Anonymous

Success is a relative term, but something all of us strive to achieve in different capacities. Some of us strive to become financially stable and independent so we can stop living from one paycheck to another and do everything we really want without worrying about the next utility bill to pay, while others are focused on living each moment to its fullest and try to seek happiness in whatever they do.

Some define success in terms of personal fulfillment and building healthy relationships whereas for some, success is all about being physically and mentally healthy. Similarly, success can hold an entirely definition for you and however all of us choose to define it, the truth is we do seek success and progress in different ways in our life.

To actualize that success, there are different things that we try. From working hard to using different technological tools to making use of the right manpower; we try to exercise every option available to us.

Unfortunately, many of us forget about the one tool all of us possess, but not all of us actually utilize to achieve the success we are so desperate to accomplish- our mind. It is a beautiful and an incredibly powerful tool whose power, if we realize and harness, can help us materialize anything we ever want. This is backed by science and is not just a theory, but reality. If we only tap into the power of our subconscious mind and harness even some of it, we can be an incredibly powerful version of ourselves and can do things we would have never dreamt of.

Yes, all of that is possible and like the quote above suggests, you can put your success on autopilot by simply switching on your ability to make your subconscious mind work as desired.

Are you interested in learning more about that? Well, if you do, this book is a detailed guide on the power of the subconscious mind and will guide you on how to tame, reprogram and control your subconscious mind to do exactly as desired.

Let's get started then and begin the journey to a new, happier you.

Table of Contents

Deciphering The Power Of The Subconscious Mind

'What I gave out in the form of words would return to me as experiences.'- Louise L. Hay

The different experiences that you encounter in life are not always sudden and because of your good or back luck, however you choose to define it. Those experiences are a manifestation of your thoughts and feelings, and no matter how much you deny it, your subconscious mind does have quite a role to play in that. Intrigued?

Your intrigue here is legit, but it also shows how oblivious you are to your own power; a power locked inside you waiting for you to tap into it. A power so strong that it can beautifully transform your life, and a power that has been given to you so you live an empowered life.

This power is possessed by your subconscious mind and while many people believe it to be something you cannot unleash, it is quite a doable task and just requires you to comprehend how your mind functions.

The Conscious, Unconscious and Subconscious Minds

It is indeed a difficult task to define explicitly the subconscious mind as your conscious and subconscious minds are most interplaying and may feel to you as one.

Your mind functions on 3 main levels. Your conscious mind is the state that you actively use when you do anything with full awareness. It is what you put to use when you are actively participating in a conversation, while reading, cooking and doing anything else with complete consciousness.

While your conscious mind is in charge of things you do with complete awareness, the truth is you aren't always working with 100% consciousness. Your mind does function on autopilot and if you observe the way you carry out many of your tasks, you will realize that several times, you function mechanically.

For instance, when driving a car, you may unintentionally apply the brakes when it is time to stop at a red traffic signal. While you are consciously seeing the traffic light turn red, your foot automatically hits the brake pedal without you even making that decision consciously.

Similarly, when you enter your house, you may unconsciously leave your shoes out at the door, change into your house slippers and close the door behind your back. You may then move towards your bathroom and put dirty clothes in the laundry as you do every single day.

You are so accustomed to this routine that you may not realize what tasks you engage in consciously. Only when you go through the list with complete attention that you acknowledge what you have been doing.

While you work on these tasks in the present moment, you may not be present while doing them. This happens because your subconscious mind has made you nurture habits of these tasks and makes you function on autopilot to save your time, energy and effort.

Your conscious mind engages in activities based on the efforts of your unconscious and subconscious minds, which are the other two states your mind operates in. Your unconscious mind stores all the information you have picked on over the years including all your fears, all the things you have tasted, every interaction you have had and everything else in between.

Your unconscious mind is indeed a huge storehouse of information and to prevent information overload, your subconscious mind picks out the most important memories and information based on how emotionally involved you were in certain situations, how much you repeat certain instances and how much something means to you.

It stores the recently formed memories and creates a program of how you should work based on all the information locked in your unconscious mind. If you were fond of balloons when you were young and have been buying balloons regularly since then, your subconscious mind makes you nurture a fondness towards balloon. If you have been drinking a glass of water regularly since you were 12, your subconscious mind picks up that information and uses it to create that habit.

Likewise, it picks the beliefs, ideas, viewpoints, fears, inhibitions, doubts and sentiments you strongly believe in and then use them to build your program. If you have been smoking for a while and feel it helps you cope with stress, your subconscious will make you nurture that belief.

That said, if you think you can overcome any addiction you have, you will have precisely that belief and you will have quite a strong willpower courtesy of that belief and the program created by your subconscious mind based on it.

Throughout the day, your subconscious collects data and sorts through it to check if you need it at any time in the future. It stores information for some time and if you don't come back looking for it, It then tosses it out in the unconscious mind. Every piece of information you have ever picked up on is in your unconscious mind and if you wish to dig it out, you can do so by putting your subconscious mind to use.

The Power of the Subconscious Mind

To succeed in life, do things you aspire to do, manifest all your ambitions and push yourself to do your best, all you need to do is to harness the subconscious mind's power.

While you cannot control all the external factors and events, you encounter, you can definitely control and manage your thoughts and your perception of events and it is this perception that helps you turn even the most unfavorable events to your favor.

Your subconscious as already stated above builds your internal program, which makes you react and respond to different things in different ways. When it picks up from your unconscious mind that you have mostly chickened out of doing things that feel tough for you, it makes you nurture the belief that you cannot overcome your fears.

It is important to point out that your thoughts travel out in the universe and draw towards them other thoughts vibrating on a similar frequency. Everything in the universe is composed of energy and has a certain vibration that it exudes at all times. Things that share a similar vibration are drawn towards one another, which is why the saying goes 'like attracts like.'

Yes, even we human beings exude a certain energy and vibration, which is through our thoughts, emotions and feelings. These feelings and thoughts travel out in the universe and interact with other thoughts and emotions. Those that vibrate at a similar frequency then mingle and are drawn towards each other.

Every thought is accompanied by a host of events, experiences, ideas, concepts and people associated to them. Hence, when a couple of thoughts interact, they bring closer all the other factors and elements associated with them.

When you come across someone at a social situation who is as passionate about plantation and is a staunch environmentalist like you, it is because your thoughts and those of that person met somewhere in the universe and had a ball of their own. They then bring you and the other person together because the two of you share the same energy and vibration.

Similarly, everything that you feel is drawn towards you happens because of the thoughts brewed up by your subconscious. All the good experiences you encounter and all the not so happy ones are also brought closer to your by your thoughts.

If you keep thinking about how bad things will happen to you, eventually you will face them. Remember the time when you kept thinking about how terrible your job interview would go and you did end up making a fool of yourself. Also, recall the time when you were sure that you would get your house mortgage approved and even though your credit history was not too good, you knew you had to get it because you had been saving for your house.

Think of other similar events, when you were and were not so positive on certain outcomes. You will be surprised to learn that your confidence and inhibitions did make you experience outcomes according to your expectations.

All of this happens because of the ramifications of your subconscious mind, and if you do wish to change certain outcomes and experiences for yourself, you only need to reprogram this wonderful creation.

How Things Can be Different if You Harness the Power of Your Subconscious Mind

Oftentimes in life, things don't go as you want them to. You plan on working for 12 hours a day because you need to earn more to achieve your goal of being financially independent, but you end up binge watching movies on Netflix for 6 hours and all you do later is to regret this. The next day you plan to work better, but your old friend shows up after 6 months and you decide to spend time with her instead.

Different external factors keep coming your way and instead of deflecting them, you keep caving in to your temptations. While you wish to respond better to such events, you end up only reacting to them by surrendering to the different distractions.

Then there are traumatic events, which often take a toll on your body and mind, and exhaust you to the core. Sometimes, you get back up sooner than you expected, but other times, you just give in to the pain and let it wash you over.

All such events, temptations, distractions and sad episodes weaken you from within and keep you from making the choices you actually wanted to take. They keep you from realizing and unleashing your power from within.

Fortunately, you can change all of that and reclaim your life by simply reprogramming your subconscious mind to think, feel and behave differently. This takes a lot of courage, strength, patience and persistence, but if you keep trying, you can achieve your goal.

You begin by setting certain targets and consciously making yourself respond to things differently. Therefore, if you feel doubtful of your ability to do something, you keep telling yourself how you can accomplish the target and you remind yourself of your strength and capability. A few tries help you nurture that habit and in a couple of weeks, you start feeling confident about yourself.

You then consciously pull yourself out of the negativity and compel your subconscious mind to create a new program, one that suits your motive and helps you achieve your goals.

If your goal is to work for 16 hours, you observe your behavior pattern and temptations and tactfully pull yourself out of the distractions and focus on your end goal. It takes a great deal of self-control to do that, but you manage to achieve it by thinking positively and employing other strategies that help you channelize the subconscious mind's true ability.

By slowly reprogramming your subconscious mind, soon enough you unleash its full power and open your treasure chest that had been lying locked for all this time.

You can then harness the power to do anything you want. From losing weight to sleeping better at night to eating healthy to quitting smoking to becoming optimistic to interacting better with people to becoming an eloquent speaker to fulfilling your goal of becoming a body builder to starting your music school to let go of your fears that hold you back to overcome depression to absolutely anything you have ever wanted to do. Even the sky stops being a limit because you know you can do it and prove it to yourself.

You realize that nothing can hold you back, and the only limitation you ever had in your life was the negativity and fear you had been fixating on all your life. All you needed to do was believe in your power and work on becoming empowered from within because it is precisely that element you need to unleash your subconscious mind's true power. As the below quote states,

'Your subconscious influences your attitude and actions, and gives you insights and solutions. To understand how yours influences you, become more conscious of your subconscious.

The journey to reprogramming your subconscious mind does begin with awareness. Now that you are aware of what your subconscious can do for you, you need to equip yourself with the ability to effectively control and reprogram it. The following chapters equip you with strategies to accomplish that.

Awareness is the Key

"We must realize that the subconscious mind is the law of action and always expresses what the conscious mind has impressed on it. What we regularly entertain in our mind creates a conception of self. What we conceive ourselves to be, we become." --Grace Speare

Whatever you frequently plant in your subconscious mind, it nourishes that seed and grows it into a plant. That said, oftentimes we engage in this activity quite unconsciously. We may not even be aware of what we are thinking or how that one simple thought is affecting our personality, behavior and life.

Similarly, we may not be aware of the many practices and activities we are actively engaged in that are not affecting us very positively. To pull yourself out of certain activities or encourage yourself to become engaged in other activities, you first need to be aware of what you are doing wrong and what you need to do in its place.

You need to realize your mistakes and shortfalls so you can then actively work on them in the right way, and you must be aware of the improvements you wish to bring in your life so you can then plan accordingly for them.

Awareness is indeed the key to tame and control your subconscious mind because unless you are not aware of the things that are not moving in the right direction and the changes you desire to bring, you will not be able to set yourself on the right track.

To move towards better things in life, you need to first inculcate the awareness you need to understand what is wrong and what you want.

Become Aware of Your Deepest and Genuine Desires

To shape your life the way you want it to be, first understand what is it you want from your life. Quite often, we chase things we *only* think we want, but don't aspire for genuinely. You may think you want a BMW, but in actuality, you may still be happy with your old Honda and really yearn for inner peace.

To make your subconscious draw the right things towards you, you need to be first clear on your wants and ambitions yourself. Unless you have the clarity of what you want, you will never get the desired outcomes. You may be getting things close to what you want, but you will never be truly satisfied because you don't receive what you want. You may keep blaming your fate for that, but the truth is you don't have complete clarity of your goals. To make your subconscious mind focus completely on your goals, first figure them out yourself.

Sit somewhere peaceful, probably somewhere, you feel relaxed and can think deeply and ponder on your heart's deepest and most genuine desires. Think of the life you wish to live and how you wish to be as a person. Take one thing at a time and get clarity on that.

Start with an area that you are most concerned about, which is mostly finance for most people. Think of how much money you would like to earn and what things you think you need to change for that outcome.

Will you be happy earning $5,000 a month or do you need $50,000? What exactly is it that you want and what changes do you think you will need to bring to accomplish them?

Keep thinking of different aspects and factors one by one and really dig deeper into what you want. Also, ponder on the type of person you wish to be. Do you want to be more disciplined, focused, relaxed, carefree, happier, confident or something else? How do you really want to see yourself and what do you think holds you back from being that person? Write down all your findings or record them on your phone/MP3. It is important to have a record that you can go through frequently to gain more clarity.

Write down in detail everything you feel is not right in your life and all the things you wish to replace the undesirable things, situations and experiences with. From your addictions to bad habits to the constant stress, you experience to your inability to socialize with people to your constant surrendering to procrastination and to everything else, you are not pleased with.

Also, write down how you wish to improve on these things and go through the lists a few times to ensure you have jotted down everything you genuinely want.

Meditate Regularly

Practiced for centuries and being vouched by generations, meditation is an incredibly effective practice that reprograms your subconscious, helps create a sense of stillness and tranquility in your mind and helps you to better understand your thoughts, aspirations and desires.

Oftentimes, we become confused about our desires and aspirations, and chase things we only think we want instead of following what we really want. This only creates chaos in our life and takes us away from our actual goals.

This is also rooted in the fact that our mind is full of thoughts, many of which aren't even our own. On average, 50,000 different kinds of thoughts run through a person's mind. Even if you filter out 50% of these thoughts, you would still have 25,000 thoughts orbiting your mind. Even that's quite a lot to think about. Amidst a plethora of thoughts, it is quite difficult to ponder on exactly what your heart yearns.

Fortunately, meditation offers you an escape from a frantic state of mind and helps you think peacefully on one thought at a time and dig deeper into its root cause. It relaxes your racing mind, helps slow down your thoughts and gives you a break from the frenzy going on inside your head so you can focus on exactly what you want.

If you build the habit of meditating daily, you would find it very easy to think about your ambitions and deepest desires and think exactly on what you want. It makes your subconscious receptive to your goals enabling it to concentrate on exactly what you want.

While there are countless ways to meditate, here is an extremely simple and effective one that works well for beginners.

- Sit comfortably in any pose you like in a quiet spot and close your eyes.

- Slowly and very gently bring your awareness to your breath and start observing it very gently.

- Inhale from your nose and watch your breath as it enters your nostrils, circulates inside your body and then observe it calmly as it leaves through your mouth when you exhale.

- It can be a little hard to observe your breath very calmly and with complete focus particularly because you do not have the habit of doing so. To make the task easier, observe the different rhythmic movements your breath produces in your body. If you observe calmly, you will be surprised to notice many movements that you were otherwise oblivious to. You will observe your tummy rising and falling, tingling sensation in your chest, slight movements in your abdomen and other such movements.

- Keep observing your breath closely for 5 to 10 minutes, or keep the practice restricted to 2 minutes if even 5 minutes is a lot for you.

- During this time, you will wander off in thought multiple times and may even feel agitated because of this. Remember to be calm and patient with yourself in this time and bring back your attention to your thoughts every time you feel distracted. This will go on for a while maybe even a few sessions, but if you consistently keep re-aligning your focus on your breath, you will soon reach the point where you can concentrate on your breath for quite a long time.

- Keep consistent at this practice and do it twice daily. In a few weeks, you will find it very easy to focus on your breath and then one thought at a time. That is the time when you should pick any one thought you would like to dig deeper into to gain more awareness into yourself and your goals. Think about yourself, your personality, things you want to do, your strengths, the purpose of your life and other aspects you feel strongly about, and write down all your findings. You then need to join the different pieces together to figure out your genuine needs, wants and ambitions.

It can take you some time to gain awareness into yourself, but if you spend an hour with your thoughts daily and meditate regularly, you will reach that point.

Pick One Improvement in Each Area

Once you have better clarity on what your heart yearns for, pick out any two to three areas of your life you would like to improve first, areas that are extremely important to you and those that you feel your life is pivoted on.

For instance, if you are fed up with your smoking addiction and are struggling with living healthy, these could be the areas you could work on to live a better life.

You then need to pinpoint the one or two specific changes you wish to achieve in those areas to improve them and live better. If you aren't happy with your finances, make a commitment to improve.

'Commitment' is the catchword here so you need to really commit yourself to the goal. Prior to doing that, you need to first create a goal based on the change you would like to accomplish.

Make a Goal and Commit Yourself to it

Goals solidify your commitment to change and serve as a reminder to your subconscious. Your subconscious mind believes whatever you tell it with conviction so if you create a goal and commit yourself to it by convicting yourself to it, your subconscious embraces your conviction and makes you focus on it.

If you decide to work on achieving financial freedom, specify how much money you aspire to make and how long will it take you to reach the finish line. There always has to be a deadline attached to your goal so you know when it is due and instead of procrastinating to work on it, get started with it right away.

If you aim to increase your monthly income from $10,000 to $50,000 in 6 months, your goal could be: 'By October 2019, I will be earning $50,000 every month.'

This is just the first half of your goal. Here, you need to specify what service you will offer in exchange of the goal. The universe is extremely gracious and does send amazing things your way if you ask for it, but it is also fair and does not do that without asking you for something in return. If you wish to achieve a certain goal, there is something you need to be willing to offer in exchange as well. So what is it that you are ready to offer the universe in order to make $50,000 every month?

At this point, think of any of your strength, talent, capability or skill that you can offer in exchange of the goal you would like to accomplish. If you are good at providing social media marketing services, you could say, 'By October 2019, I will be earning $50,000 every month by offering social media marketing services to the best of my abilities.'

Similarly, whatever goal you have, identify the things you would be willing to do in exchange for it. If your goal is to overcome alcoholism, you could say, 'By December 2019, I will have overcome my alcohol addiction by meditating regularly and taking therapy.' Remember, there has to be something you would have to do in order to enjoy a certain accomplishment.

Once you have set your goal, commit yourself to it by chanting it aloud. Speak out that goal repeatedly, and while writing it simultaneously to convict your subconscious to it. When you do accomplish this goal, you can set another one picking the next area of your life you wish to improve and then keep working on one positive goal after another.

To accomplish the goal you have just set, create a detailed plan of action to dedicatedly work towards achieving that goal. However, to ensure you do that successfully and effectively, you need to make your subconscious mind believe that you are capable of achieving the goal and can do so successfully. The next chapter educates you on how to do that so that you make your subconscious mind embrace your commitment and become sincere to it.

Make Your Subconscious Mind Embrace Your Goal

'The subconscious mind is ruled by suggestion, it accepts all suggestions- it does not argue with you- it fulfills all your wishes.'- Dr. Joseph Murphy

Your subconscious mind indeed responds effectively to suggestions, be it positive, negative or neutral. Whatever you tell it with complete conviction, it accepts that. The truth is it is designed in a manner that it cannot distinguish between reality and imagination. It accepts whatever you throw its way with conviction. This is both, favorable and unfavorable for you and depends largely on what suggestions you choose to believe in and repeatedly tell yourself.

This is the reason why you have not been able to achieve your goal of becoming physically healthy and mentally peaceful because you kept suggesting to yourself the wrong things over the years. You kept telling yourself how difficult it is to exercise and follow your fitness regimen and how you cannot let go of your painful past because it keeps haunting you. You fixated on all these things repeatedly, which is why you only achieved unhappy and undesirable outcomes.

If only you had made your subconscious mind embrace the right and positive suggestions and convicted yourself to them, you would have achieved exactly what you wanted. If only you had reminded yourself of your goal and told yourself how you can fight your temptations and become fit, healthy and active, you would have accomplished it. If only you would have chosen to let go of your painful memories and dedicated yourself to only being happy, you would have been happy and peaceful.

So what if you couldn't do that in all this time, you can still achieve it and it is doable. You can fulfill all your goals and live a life you have always desired to live. All you need to do for that is to make your subconscious mind accept your goal and shift its attention towards your desired goal. Once it embraces your positive goal completely, it will only create positive thoughts in that direction and make you act accordingly.

Here are some strategies you can employ to achieve that:

Visualize Yourself Achieving the Goal

Visualization is an incredibly effective technique that employs creative imagery to make your subconscious mind feel that you have achieved a goal you wish to accomplish. When you repeatedly visualize yourself fulfilling a certain goal, you affirm that goal to it and make it feel that it is your reality. Here it is important to mention the RAS in your brain. Reticular activating system is a system in the brain created to prevent information overload.

If you commit all the information you pick up to your long-term memory, your brain would suffer from information overload and become exhausted. Your mental wellbeing and cognition would suffer as a result which would only make it difficult for you to function healthily and successfully. To keep this from happening, the RAS is created so it filters out all the unnecessary information out from your conscious realization and makes you focus on only the important things.

When you repeatedly chant a suggestion or focus on a scenario by visualizing it, you activate your RAS and make your subconscious mind active towards that information. Hence, when you visualize yourself accomplishing a certain goal and practice that visualization repeatedly, you activate your RAS's focus towards that goal and become committed to it. This then increases your focus towards it and makes you create thoughts centered on it, which then draw positive experiences your way. This is how positive affirmations (the method discussed below) works as well.

To practice visualization, sit in a peaceful room and close your eyes. Think of your goal that you would like to achieve and without thinking of how you would reach the destination, imagine yourself achieving it.

If your goal is to overcome your alcohol addiction, close your eyes and think that you have eventually reached the day when you no longer are dependent on booze to feel relaxed and feel happy, confident and peaceful without it. You feel good about yourself and don't need even an ounce of alcohol to do anything. While imagining that scenario, engage all your senses in the practice to become completely involved in it and commit your subconscious completely to the practice.

Imagine how happy and elated you feel; sense the happy expressions you feel on your face; focus on any taste you can feel in your mouth; and concentrate on the odor you can smell. Keep thinking about that scenario and focus on the tiniest of details such as the color of the clothes you are wearing that day, the people you are surrounded by and the feelings you experience. A good idea is to write down the things you visualize to become even more engrossed in the practice.

You now need to practice this visualization for at least 15 minutes twice daily to commit your subconscious to it. You will be surprised at how committed you become to your goal within a matter of weeks and before you realize it, you will witness amazing things coming your way that would only take you closer to your goal.

Practice Positive Affirmations

Another practice you can engage in to further strengthen your commitment is to practice positive affirmations daily. Firstly, you need to chant the goal you created earlier 10 times twice daily and write it down at least thrice and then you need to chant positive affirmations based on it. If your goal is to become financially free, say 'I am financially free and strong, and wealth flows easily towards me.'

Remember to create a purely positive goal that must not contain a single negative word in it including 'no', 'not', 'cannot' and 'don't because your subconscious cannot recognize these words and omits them from suggestion, and then rephrases them. If you say, 'I will not smoke cigarettes', your subconscious is likely to change the suggestion to 'I will smoke cigarettes.' To better understand this, think of the last time you were told not to do something and you did precisely what you were asked not to.

To ensure your subconscious focuses on the right goal, set a positive goal only. If you wish to quit alcohol, say, 'I have overcome my alcohol addiction.' Also, keep the suggestion present oriented, which means it should suggest you have achieved your goal. Instead of saying, 'I will be a millionaire', chant 'I am a millionaire.' Present oriented goals make your subconscious focus on the goal right now and increase your commitment, as your subconscious cannot differentiate between reality and imagination. Therefore, when your subconscious feels you have achieved something now, it reinforces your commitment and makes you work harder towards it, and draws positive experiences your way in the present moment.

Practice positive affirmations by speaking them out very loudly, clearly and confidently so every word rings in your ears and you become completely focused on it. Do this regularly and religiously just as you eat a couple of meals or even more every day. Make it a part of your routine and within days, you will be surprised at how positive you feel from within and how motivated you become to bring positive improvements in your life.

Anchor Confidence to Your Subconscious

To stay strong in difficult times and bring your awareness back to your goals every time a bout of self-doubt attacks you, learn to anchor confidence, happiness, peace and positivity to your subconscious.

Anchoring is an extremely useful NLP (neuro-linguistic programming) technique that enables you to imbed positive emotions into your subconscious mind by anchoring them to a physical gesture. Every time you practice that gesture, your subconscious is directed to give you a nice boost of the respective positive emotion so you experience it and behave accordingly.

If you anchor confidence to a finger snap, every time you snap your fingers, you will feel confident from within and be able to fight the self-doubt brimming inside you. This technique rewires your subconscious to behave as desired so you experience desired outcomes and work committed towards your goals.

There will be times during the journey when you will feel scared, doubtful, unconfident, negative and depressed. You cannot control external influences and factors, and every journey is adorned with some obstacles so there will be times when you will doubt your ability to move forward, reconsider the pursuit of your goal and will want to quit.

In all such times, it is important to learn to trust yourself again and direct your subconscious mind towards your goal.

Anchoring is a technique that helps you combat those difficult times by helping you feel confident, happy, safe, peaceful and determined with just a simple gesture.

To practice anchoring, here is what you should do:

- Think of an emotion you would like to anchor for now, say confidence for instance. You can later anchor multiple emotions to multiple gestures respectively and enjoy them from time to time.

- Pick a gesture you would like to anchor that emotion to. Choose a simple gesture that is easy to remember and practice.

- Now think of the emotion you wish to anchor and any time in your life when you experienced it to the fullest. For instance, if you would like to anchor confidence, think of the time when you felt extremely confident and play that memory in your head.

- Rewind that memory, play it from the start, and slowly take it to the point when you felt extremely self-confident. Visualize that picture in your head and recall feeling incredibly self-assured. When you feel your confidence rising to 100%, practice the gesture you wish to anchor the confidence to. If you want to anchor it to a finger snap, snap three fingers and imagine feeling extremely confident in that memory.

- Replay that memory a couple of times and every time you reach the point where you felt super-poised, practice the finger snap. Doing it about 4 to 5 times is mostly enough to anchor the emotion and gesture together.

- Now think of something completely unrelated and practice the gesture. If you have anchored confidence to it successfully, you will feel extremely confident instantly.

Practice this technique regularly to master it and then use it to anchor different emotions to your subconscious mind so you can experience them when the need arises. Soon, you will know how to feel happy, relaxed, confident, strong and patient with a simple gesture and would easily get yourself back on track every time you are tricked by self-doubt.

All these tactics engage your subconscious mind and help you reprogram it just the way you want. That said, your subconscious needs to believe you can do all of the things you reprogram it for and that happens only when you provide it with reliable proof. You need to prove your subconscious you can do all of the things you reprogram it to think about. The next chapter guides you on how to accomplish that.

Working Towards Your Goals To Make Your Subconscious Work Harder Towards Their Fulfillment

Accomplishments help your subconscious mind understand that you are capable of doing all that you have been affirming it. When your subconscious sees proof of your abilities, skills, talents and strengths, it embraces your affirmations even better and places all its faith on them. This helps strengthen the new positive program you are trying to create inside you so you can successfully actualize all your goals.

Also, as you achieve different milestones and goals one after another, your self-esteem starts to improve. Your self-esteem refers to how much you value yourself and is based on how you perceive yourself. If you have a positive self-image, your self-esteem is likely to be high as well. Your self-image is dependent on how much you value yourself, which relies on the accomplishments you have to your credit. When you actualize your goals, you feel good about yourself, which slowly increases your self-esteem.

As your self-esteem increases, it boosts your confidence and when you feel self-assured, you find it easier to find the courage to set bigger targets, push yourself harder and set out on journeys you have been meaning to embark on for ages.

Doing things that you wanted and achieving your goals proves that you are capable of doing all that you have been reprogramming your subconscious for which only increases your strength, self-discipline and grit. To achieve that, you need to get started with actively pursuing your goals.

Here's how you can do that:

Break Your Goal into Weekly Incremental Goals

Willpower is what you need to effectively work on your action plan. You need to practice self-control every time you feel giving in to your temptations. You need to stay positive when negativity hits you hard. You need to keep your subconscious focused on your goals so you don't lose sight of them and keep working consistently towards them. You need to remind yourself of what you ought to do and what you must avoid. You need willpower and discipline to do all of this, and for that, you need to go slow and easy on yourself.

Willpower is not built overnight; it takes time, effort and a lot of consistency. More importantly, you need to go very easy on yourself and ensure you don't feel overwhelmed throughout the process.

When you set a goal and start reprogramming your subconscious to achieve it, you will feel overwhelmed. As excited and happy as you will be to bring a monumental change in your life, you will be equally overwhelmed and may feel the urge to quit the pursuit after some days.

Your subconscious needs proof to make you work towards your goals and the proof cannot be produced if you lose your motivation just after a few days of working hard or just thinking positively. This is where 'breaking down your goal into smaller, doable milestones' comes in handy. A big goal is naturally going to exhaust you emotionally and dampen your spirits. Naturally, if you are asked to wash 100 dishes, you will feel swamped even thinking about it. However, if you are asked to wash 10 dishes first and then do 10 more after a short break, you will feel less burdened.

The same applies to goal setting and pursuing your targets. Instead of seeing your goal as one, enormous task, break it down into smaller chunks. You need to have weekly incremental goals instead of a gigantic goal spread over a couple of months to a year.

If your goal is to earn a certain amount of money in 6 months, define how much you expect to make each week. For instance, if you wish to save $50,000 in 6 months, you could set a goal to save $500 to $1000 every week and increase your earnings by 20% every 4 weeks.

If your goal is to work for 12 hours a day, spread it over 2 months and increase 2 hours of workload every week if you currently just work for 4 hours daily. Whatever your goal is, break it down into a mid-term and short-term goal and then chop those down into weekly incremental goals. This way you keep your motivation alive as you keep adding increments to your goal and smoothly move towards it.

Define Tasks and Steps

Next, you have to define the different tasks and steps you need to execute to achieve each weekly incremental goal. If your weekly target is to cut back on your alcohol consumption and drink only 5 glasses a day from 8 during the week, what do you propose to do to achieve this? Every time your temptation attacks, how do you plan to block it. What other activities do you plan to engage in if not drinking booze? What are your different tasks assigned for the day and how do you plan to execute them?

Similarly, if your weekly target is to land a client for your insurance company that buys insurance worth of $10,000 at least, what tasks do you intend to carry out to achieve that? Are you going to attend more social meet-ups to meet more people? Are you going to resort to social media to look for clients? Are you going to carry out cold calling? You need to clearly define all that you propose to do to achieve your weekly target and then detail out the tasks.

Ensure that you get into the minute details because you need to define what you will do to execute a certain task and how you will carry it out. Details are important because they help you understand the effort that is expected to be invested in a task so you are aware of the process beforehand and do not worry about it on the nick of time. Also, many people have the habit of planning right when a task is due which only wastes time. Planning beforehand saves time and keeps you from overthinking at the last minute.

Overthinking a task is just a bad habit many of us nurture which is basically an excuse to get yourself out of doing a task and procrastinate instead. It only makes you slip into analysis paralysis and take no action in the end. Spare yourself the trouble and plan your tasks and steps in detail beforehand so when it is time for you to execute a task, you just work on it and get results.

Assign High Priority Tasks Daily

When creating your tasks for the week, make sure that you set a high priority task for every day of the week. A high priority task is an important task that boosts your productivity and helps you achieve your goals faster.

For example, if your weekly target is to land a client for your marketing firm that gives you business of at least $5,000 a month, a high priority task would be to attend an upcoming important seminar where new startups and entrepreneurs are expected to show up so you can socialize with businesspeople and find potential clients.

There needs to be at least one high priority task on your plan for every day so every single day, you do something extremely meaningful to move towards your target. Also, when you accomplish something daily, you remind your subconscious of how capable you are which strengthens your focus on your goal and makes it work harder towards it.

When assigning your tasks for the day or next day, do assess each task in detail to figure out if it belongs to the 'high priority' or 'low priority' category. You already know what the former encompasses; the latter includes tasks that do not give your productivity the much-needed kick. While there are certain low priority tasks that are important for the routine functioning, if a task does not really impact the fulfillment of your goal, keep it for a time of the day when you don't have anything important to do.

Eat an Ugly Frog Every Day

Another great strategy to make your subconscious mind work effectively towards all your goals especially the purpose of your life is to eat one ugly frog every day. Okay, do not freak out, you do not actually have to do that, but just something similar, not as disgusting though. You have to work on at least one important, difficult task every day particularly in the start of the day.

Oftentimes, we keep difficult tasks for the end and later procrastinate on them completely. This influences your productivity, doesn't help in the fulfillment of your goals and also slowly weakens the new program your subconscious is trying to create. To ensure this doesn't happen to you, do one difficult task every day.

Identify all the important, seemingly difficult tasks associated with your goal and work on one every day of the week. If your goal is to overcome an addiction, the difficult task would likely be to manage your temptations. In this case, think of the different activities you can do to avoid your temptations and achieve your weekly incremental goal.

Take Action Daily

Once you create your plan of action, go through it a few times to ensure you don't miss out on an important point and after reviewing it a couple of times, start working on it.

You need to take action right away, and not miss out on a single opportunity to work. Go through the list and see what can be done right away and just do it. If you cannot tend to any high priority task, but can send an email to a potential client right away, do it.

You need to take meaningful action every single day without procrastinating on any important task so you start achieving extraordinary results. If procrastination hits you hard, anchor positivity and enthusiasm to your subconscious so you become motivated to work on your tasks and get started with them before it gets late.

Also, when you start working on your plan before wasting a minute and work on a task the minute you assign it to yourself, you train your subconscious to work actively and avoid procrastination. This is how you nurture the habit of doing work right away and beat procrastination.

Review Your Performance

As you start working on your action plan, you need to review your performance on a regular basis. When you start with a task, write down its name, details, starting time, ending time, problems you encountered in it, achievements you unlock, any strengths or weaknesses identified and how you pushed yourself to move from the start to the finish line.

Go through this analysis at the end of the day so you can assess your performance in every task throughout the day. On reviewing your performance, think of ways to overcome the problems you have identified and then implement the strategies.

For instance, if you identify that you are afraid of difficult tasks, make an effort to break it down into smaller parts and work on building skills that can help you achieve your desired results successfully.

Similarly, whatever problem areas you identify, work on managing them successfully so you can move further towards your destination.

Make Improvements to Your Plan Accordingly

Your action plan is the secret sauce to your success, but do not be too rigid about it. While you need to work on it strictly, you also need to adopt a flexible attitude towards it. When you review it and figure out problem areas in it, make improvements to it accordingly. Revisit your action plan frequently and keep adding positive changes to it to make it as effective as possible.

The journey to your goal will not start on its own. You will have to take that step yourself by working on the guidelines discussed above. During this journey, you will encounter obstacles particularly the tricks played by your mind. Fortunately, that too can be surpassed and we have just the right tricks for you to achieve it. The next chapter tells you to how to do that.

Staying Focused, Positive And Motivated Towards Your Goals

'The subconscious mind is the guiding force for your entire life.'- Kevin Michel

Your subconscious is indeed the force that can guide you towards the right direction provided you choose the right direction and stay committed to it. Your end goal can sometimes become fuzzy when you keep encountering obstacles and experience setbacks one after another.

While we have discussed some strategies to affirm positivity to your subconscious, here are some more practices that you can employ to keep your subconscious mind under your control and make it work towards your set targets.

Try the RWID Formula

The RWID formula stands for 'relative weight of importance and duration' and is quite an effectual technique to reprogram your subconscious. Your mind is programmed by thoughts that you assign more value and importance to and those that run in your head for a long time.

For instance, if you become too excited on your convocation and keep thinking about how good you felt when you received your degree, you will focus on it and will make this thought an important part of your subconscious mind's program.

To make your subconscious mind focus on the right things and thoughts that you wish to run in your mind, you need to distinguish between positive and negative thoughts, and allow the former kind to orbit your mind for a long time.

You need to actively stay aware of the negative thoughts that enter your mind and discard them away instantly. The right way to do that is by replacing them with positive thoughts instead.

Yes, getting rid of negative thoughts is difficult, but not impossible. Here is how you can implement the RWID formula and give weight to positive thoughts and allow them to reside in your mind for long so they help create your growth mindset.

- First, you need to become more mindful of your negative thoughts and all your thoughts for that matter. Being mindful means that you need to be actively aware of the different thoughts, feelings and emotions that run through your mind and system and accept them as they are without attaching any sort of labels or negativity to them. Doing this is important because unless you are aware of the thoughts that run through your mind, you won't be able to pinpoint unhealthy thoughts on time. Also, if you perceive certain thoughts as bad, you will only feel more bitter towards them. Yes, certain thoughts don't impact you positively, but you need to identify that instead of labeling them as 'bad.' When you are accepting towards certain unconstructive thoughts, you stop criticizing the thoughts and instead accept that it is their effect on you, which isn't right and you need to modify the thoughts to keep negative influences away from you. You have been taught how to practice mindfulness based breathing meditation in the previous chapter so start practicing it often to slowly gain better insight into your thoughts and improve your awareness of toxic thoughts the minute they pop in your head.

- When you identify an unconstructive thought, write it down and then analyze it for a while in an unbiased manner. For instance, if you thought 'I am not good enough', objectively assess it to understand whether it is true. Often, certain thoughts make room in your mind not because they are true, but because you focus too much on them. Before fixating on a not-so-helpful thought, assess its rationality and see whether it is authentic. So if you think you are not good enough, ponder on why you feel that way. What proof do you have that shows you aren't good enough and in what ways do you feel that way about yourself? Detail out any evidence you have that proves the authenticity of this thought and think of all the times when you did feel good about yourself and accomplished something. You need to challenge your negative thought by proving it wrong or simply showing that it isn't as genuine as you feel it is.

- Next, you need to analyze the effect of the thought before finally deciding whether to keep or discard it. Focus on the thought for a while and see how it makes you feel. If it brews up any sort of pain, resentment, grief and hurt inside you, it isn't a thought that you need to focus on for a long time. It is now time to do away with this thought and find its positive replacement.

- Write down that unhealthy thought as it is and then look for any words with a negative connotation in it such as 'no', 'not', 'never', 'cannot', 'don't', 'won't' and other similar words. Just take out those words from the suggestion and see how reading it feels. Continuing with the earlier example, omit 'not' from 'I am not good enough' and it turns into 'I am good enough.' Read this suggestion a few times out aloud and observe its effect on your mind. If it makes you feel positive and good from within, it is a positive thought and you ought to focus on it for long. Work in a similar manner on all your unconstructive thoughts and you will be surprised at how happy the new, positive thoughts make you feel. If a certain thought does not feel positive even after you take out negative words from it, replace it with another realistically positive thought. For instance, if you think 'I am going to fail at getting my loan application approved this time too', change it to 'If I file my application documents correctly and ensure to fulfill all the requirements, my application will get approved.' Ensure the suggestion is positive and realistic at the same time so your subconscious accepts it easily.

- You then need to allow that positive thought to run through your head for some time and become involved in it. Visualize yourself achieving the goal stated in the suggestion and think about it time and again. If you think about it consistently even for an entire day, it will become rooted in your mind and will shape your subconscious positively.

Work on this strategy every time you find any sort of negativity affecting your mind so you encourage your subconscious mind to focus on your goal only and stay optimistic at all times.

Exercise the Superhero Technique

The 'superhero' technique is another effective NLP technique that helps reprogram and manipulate your subconscious to think exactly how and what you want it to think. There are going to come times when you won't feel like working on your plan of action, or when you will only want to relax, or when you will feel intimidated by an obstacle that scares you. In such times, you need strength and courage, and the superhero technique can do that beautifully.

- Think of any of your favorite superheroes or any character from a movie or book with a superpower you admire a lot. If Iron Man is your favorite, think of him and his capabilities that you appreciate.

- Now think of the problem in your life that is dampening your spirits and imagine your favorite superhero in that situation. Think of how he/ she battles that problem and overcomes it in the end. Pay attention to any details in your visualization and replay this scenario in your head a few times.

- Go through this visualization a few times and imagine your favorite superhero in other problematic situations you have faced in life and see him/ her combat them successfully every time.

- Next, imagine your superhero standing in front of you. Imagine that you are stepping out of your body and slowly moving towards your superhero and step inside him/ her. Once you enter his/ her body, you become him/her and are your new favorite superhero. You can be anyone you want from Jean Grey (X-Men) to Captain America to Hermione (Harry Potter) and once you imagine yourself being in that superhero's/ super heroine's body, feel strength, power, courage, wisdom and confidence enter your being.

- How does it feel? How confident and good do you feel being in the shoes of your favorite superhero and how strong do you think you have become now? You are likely to feel quite assured, secure and amazing from within.

- You need to once again think of your problems now, one by one, and imagine that you are the one battling them now. Everything that the superhero did before is what you are doing now and are handling all your issues like a pro.

- Practice this technique a few times and you will feel extremely confident, convinced and sure of your ability to handle your problems now.

Every time you exercise this strategy, write down how it makes you feel and whether or not it actually helps you manage the problem at hand. If you work on it consistently, it will rewire your subconscious to work just the way you want.

Conclusion

The power to do everything that you ever wanted is just inside you, waiting for you to unlock it and trust me, you can do it. This book is right by your side and if you pay heed to the actionable information in it, you will only move in the right direction in life. Good luck on this journey.

I'd Love It If You <u>Leave a Review of This Book on Amazon</u>.

PSS: Let Me Also Help You Save Some Money!

If you are a heavy reader, have you considered subscribing to Kindle Unlimited? You can read this and millions of other books for just $9.99 a month)! You can check it out by searching for Kindle Unlimited on Amazon!

Made in the USA
Coppell, TX
09 September 2020